Lemon skin thief

Lee runs from the field. "Come and look at the lemon tree, Mum!" he says. "There are lemons with no skins hanging on it. Some lemons with no skins are under the tree, too."

3

"What!" says Mum.
"The lemons have no skins?"
She hurries out to the field.

"It must be a thief," Lee says.

"A thief has eaten the skins
off the lemons," says Mum.

"Is the thief Pixie, the dog next door?" Lee says.

"No! Not Pixie!" says Mum.
"Pixie would not be a thief.
This will be a pest thief."

"Could it be a rabbit thief?"
Lee says.

"It will not be a rabbit thief,"
Mum says. "We do not have
rabbits here."

"Miss Shields can tell us,"
Mum adds.

"Miss Shields! She is my
teacher! She would say,
'go on the web'," says Lee.

So Lee looks up lemon skin pests on the internet.

"The thief must be a rat!"
Lee says. "Here it is – a
rat eating lemon skins!"
So Mum sets the rat trap.

The next day, Lee looks at the trap and there is the rat thief!

"We trapped the chief thief," Lee yells, as he hurries from the field.

"Mum! We got the rat!
The lemons are safe."

Words to blend

field	thief	Shields
chief	he	she
be	we	hurries
Pixie	lemons	skins
rabbit	teacher	pests
internet	trapped	

Before reading

Synopsis: The lemons in Lee's lemon orchard have lost their skins. Where have the skins gone, and who is the thief?

Review phonemes and graphemes: /f/ ph; /w/ wh; /ai/ ay, a-e, ea, eigh, ey, aigh, a; /ee/ ea, e-e, y, ey

Focus phoneme: /ee/   **Focus graphemes:** ie, e

Story discussion: Look at the cover, and read the title together. Ask: *What kind of book do you think this is – fiction or non-fiction? Why do you think this? What do you think the lemon skin thief could be?*

Link to prior learning: Remind children that the sound /ee/ as in 'see' can also be spelled 'ie' and 'e'. Turn to page 9 and ask children to find as many words as they can with each spelling of the /ee/ sound (Pixie, be, thief).

Vocabulary check: pest: a creature that eats or attacks plants and food.

Decoding practice: Display the words 'thief', 'she', 'be' and 'hurries'. Can children circle the letter string that makes the /ee/ sound, and read each word?

Tricky word practice: Display the words 'could' and 'would'. Ask children to circle the tricky part of the words ('oul', which makes the short /oo/ sound – as in good). Practise writing and reading these words. Can they think of another tricky word with this spelling pattern? (e.g. should)

After reading

Apply learning: Discuss the book. Ask: *Why do you think the rat was stealing the lemon skins?* Let children share their ideas.

Comprehension

- What is the name of Lee's teacher? (Miss Shields)

- How did Lee find out what the lemon skin thief was? (he looked it up on the internet)

- What did Lee and Mum catch in the end? (a rat)

Fluency

- Pick a page that most of the group read quite easily. Ask them to reread it with pace and expression. Model how to do this if necessary.

- In pairs, children can read the dialogue on pages 10–11, each reading one character's speech. Encourage children to speak as though they were the characters, taking cues from context and the illustrations.

- Practise reading the words on page 17.

Tricky words review

do	come	says
there	no	are
some	what	would
out	could	my
go	have	here